Instrumental Duet Series

Book 1

Stylized Selections for Flute and Piano

Arranged by Ed Hogan and Mary Ellen Kerrick

 **PUBLISHING COMPANY**
KANSAS CITY, MO 64141

A separate flute solo folio is temporarily stapled to the center of this book.
It is easily removed by a slight outward pull.

Contents

THEMATIC MEDLEYS

4

This Is My Father's World

Traditional English Melody
Arranged by Ed Hogan and Mary Ellen Kerrick

9

For the Beauty of the Earth

CONRAD KOCHER
Arranged by Ed Hogan and Mary Ellen Kerrick

Expressively

14

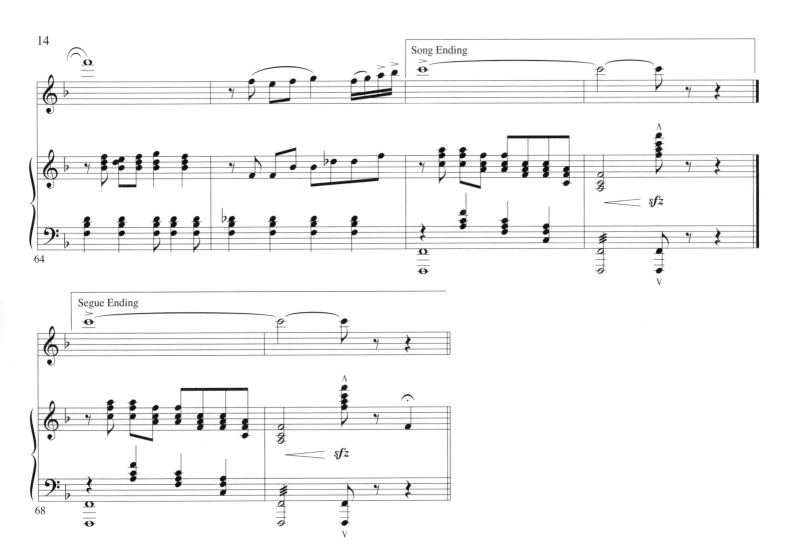

Fairest Lord Jesus

Schlesische Volkslieder
Arranged by Ed Hogan and Mary Ellen Kerrick

18

Savior, Like a Shepherd Lead Us

WILLIAM B. BRADBURY
Arranged by Ed Hogan and Mary Ellen Kerrick

23

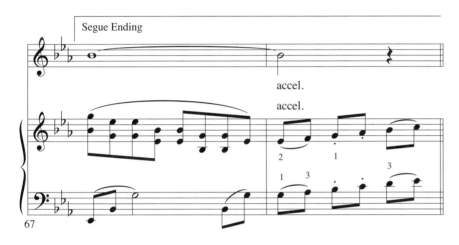

He Leadeth Me

WILLIAM B. BRADBURY
Arranged by Ed Hogan and Mary Ellen Kerrick

28

All the Way My Savior Leads Me

ROBERT LOWERY
Arranged by Ed Hogan and Mary Ellen Kerrick

The Love of God

FREDERICK M. LEHMAN
Arranged by Ed Hogan and Mary Ellen Kerrick

34

With Conviction

rit.

rit.

33

A Little Slower

Reverently (♩ = 76)

p

p

melody

37

melody

mp

41

melody

mp

46

Song Ending

Segue Ending

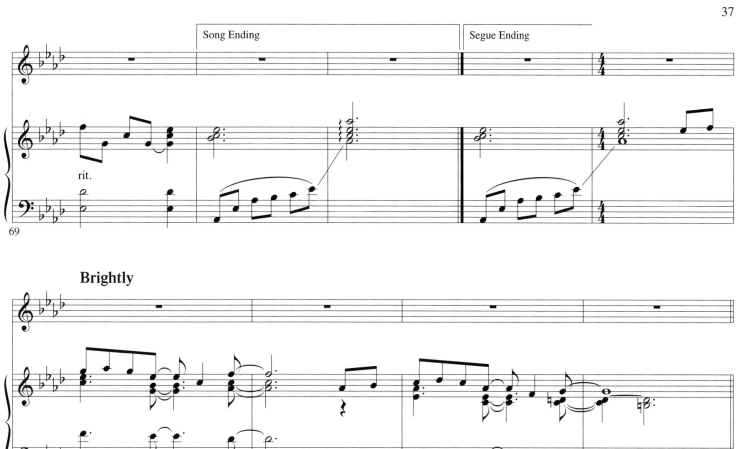

rit.

Brightly

Jesus Loves Me

WILLIAM B. BRADBURY
Arranged by Ed Hogan and Mary Ellen Kerrick

My Savior's Love

CHARLES H. GABRIEL
Arranged by Ed Hogan and Mary Ellen Kerrick

Tempo Primo

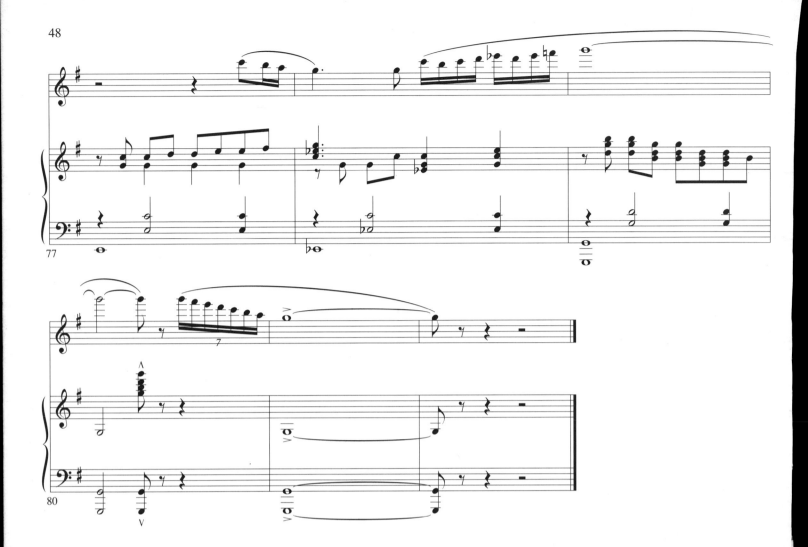